Mommy, who is God?

Written by
Cathleen Groteluschen

Illustrations by
Evgenia Dolotovskaia

For my children whom inspire me.

Christian, Summer, Hailey, Jaden, and Averi.

Love you, Mom

Mommy, who is God?

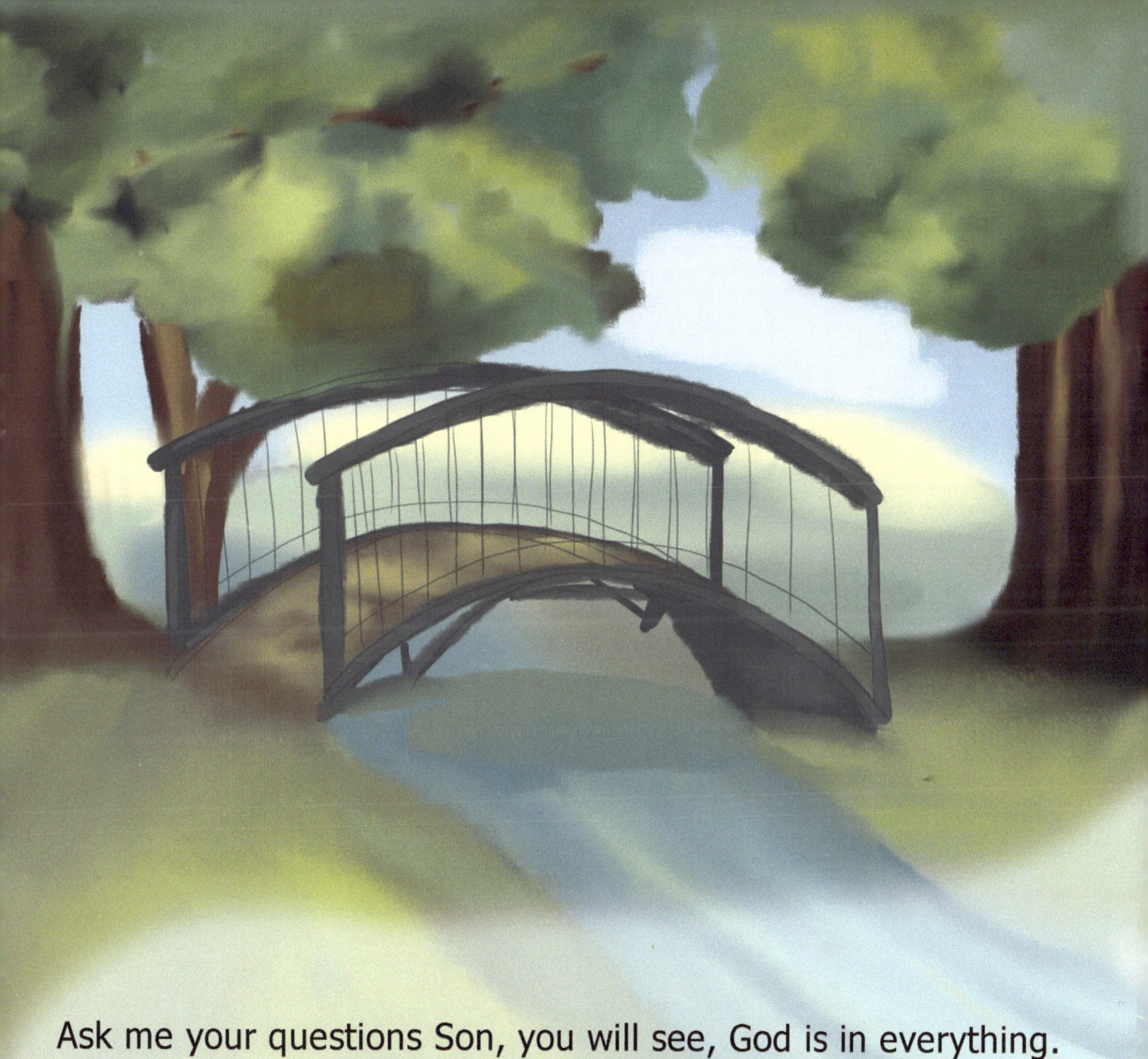

Ask me your questions Son, you will see, God is in everything.

God is a part of you as well as a part of me.

Mommy, why are we not able to see God?

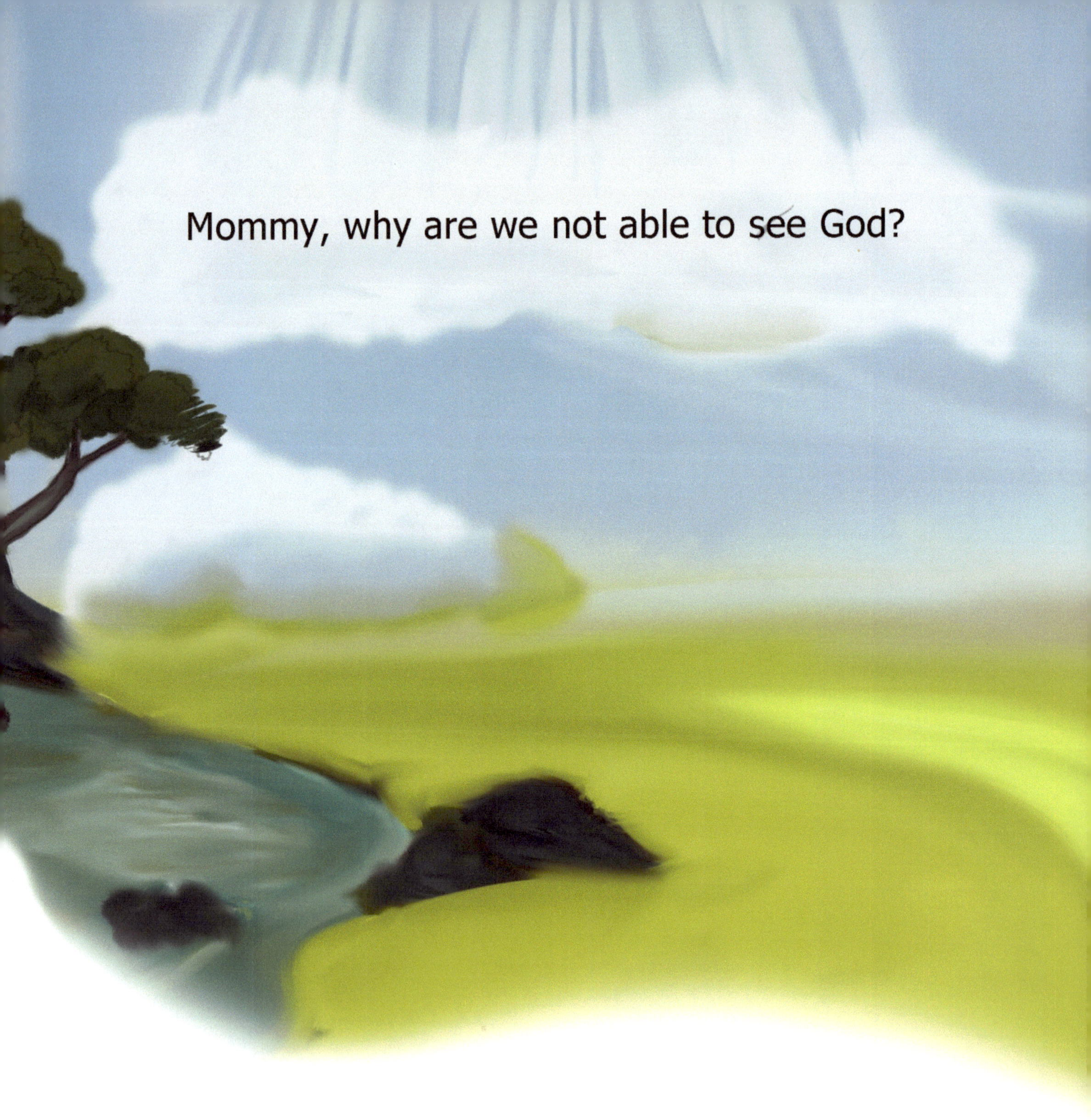

Dear child a question to ponder.

God is so powerful you see we must look for him in

creations that he has made. We may see

God in the beauty of people, places, and things.

Mom, why do you think we are not able to touch God?

God is so grand and so mighty we don't touch him because he is without a body.

Mommy, how do I know that God loves me?

HOSPITAL ✚

We have been created from God's love, unselfishly.

He has filled us with his love and gifted us opportunities.

God, knows we are not perfect, but loves us unconditionally.

Wow, I love God so much mom!

How does God know that I love him?

When we do for others and for the earth Son, we do for God.

Do you remember when you stayed with the neighbor girl Avery, after she fell from her bicycle? You stayed with Avery until her mommy could get to her.

"Yes, I remember."

That shows God your love and compassion for others,

there is no more honorable way to show

God our love for him, than by helping neighbors.

God, I pray to keep me safe and fill me with your grace.

Please watch over my family

and let them feel your sweet embrace. Amen.

God is everywhere, in everything.

Always listening.

God is loving you through the good things that you do.

God is a part of you and a part of me too.

My Journal

My name is _____

I am _____ years old

 Who is God? _____

_____

_____

Why do you think that we can not see God? _____

_____

_____

_____

Would you say that we can touch God? _____

_____

_____

_____

How do you hear God? _____

_____

_____

_____

_____

How do you know that God loves you? _____

_____

_____

_____

_____

How does God know that you love him? _____

_____

_____

_____

If you wanted to get in touch with God, how might you do that? _____

_____

_____

_____

Write a letter to God

_____

_____

_____

_____

_____

_____

_____

_____

_____

_____

_____

_____

_____

_____

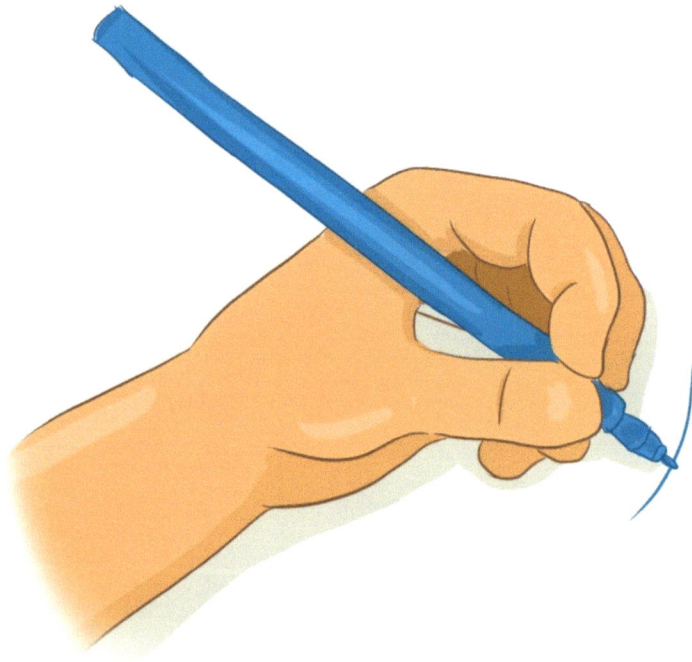

Draw a picture for God

www.ingramcontent.com/pod-product-compliance
Lightning Source LLC
Chambersburg PA
CBHW042108040426
42448CB00002B/186